Love
Eternal

LAURA MILLER

Balboa Press books may be ordered through booksellers or by contacting:

Balboa Press
A Division of Hay House
1663 Liberty Drive
Bloomington, IN 47403
www.balboapress.com
844-682-1282

ISBN: 978-1-9822-7120-6 (sc)
978-1-9822-7122-0 (hc)
978-1-9822-7121-3 (e)

Library of Congress Control Number: 2021913683

Print information available on the last page.

Balboa Press rev. date: 11/15/2021

BALBOA.PRESS
A DIVISION OF HAY HOUSE

Love
Eternal

A True Love Story of Puffy and Me

Written By:

LAURA DIANE MILLER

TABLE OF CONTENTS

INTRODUCTION

Love is love, whether between human and human, or human and reptile.
This is not your usual love story, nor is it about an ordinary love. This
book is about a very unique one of a kind green iguana.
He was perfect for me, and his name was Puffy.
Puffy puffed himself up to show off and impress people. That is why I named him Puffy.
I consider owning Puffy, and just how tuned in he was to
me, nothing short of a miracle and a blessing.
I am grateful and privileged to have enjoyed him for 17 beautiful years.
In these chapters, I will go over Puffy's extraordinary personality, his diet,
our routines together, and how I did my best to care for him.
Puffy, being the great guy he was, gave me a reason for living and made my life worth living.

CHAPTER ONE

The Best Day of My Life

I met Puffy in an exotic animal pet store in Central Florida. The day was September 27th, 2003. The minute Puffy and I saw each other, we both knew it was right! Puffy was the only iguana in a tank of around 50 or more just like him. What made it interesting was that Puffy was the only iguana in that tank that communicated with me instantly.

He was sitting off by himself. And used facial expressions and body language to talk to me. Puffy closed and opened his eyes a lot, showing signs of contentment seeing me. He had an expression of happiness on his face. My first impression was, "here's the perfect pet for me!" He's looking for someone who will love him and be with him, someone to talk to him and tuck him in at night. He was waiting for someone like me, who will treat him as more than just a lizard to be kept in a cage.

Iguanas, given a chance will show us just how intelligent they are, and yes, they do understand words! Puffy showed me just how intuitive and sensitive he was on our very first meeting in the pet store; I learned his methods of communicating with me. Puffy had a cage set up for him at home. This is important when bringing an iguana home, so he can feel secure, grow properly, and stay healthy. The cage was made out of wire mesh, 2"x2"'s with metal hinges for the door. A few shelves of wood were available to him, along with a log to climb on. He had a food dish, which was a white seashell, a water dish and most importantly, a UVB fixture and bulb. This was placed on a screen made of wire on top of the cage. A heat bulb and fixture were also placed on top of the cage.

Iguanas get warmed up from the air temperature and from UVB light. UVB is ultraviolet light that an iguana needs to process calcium in his body. The sun is the best source of the UVB rays an iguana needs. Puffy's cage was near a window; the window was open at times to let the sunlight in. Puffy also had a sun cage built into the kitchen window. He had a custom made wooden ladder going up into the kitchen countertop. This enabled Puffy to go in and out for real sunshine whenever he wanted to.

As tame as he was at the start, Puffy quickly became a "free roamer" around the house. He would go back by himself to his cage to sleep. A lot of times after exploring the house, he would climb up to the top of his cage for forty winks during the daytime. From the pet store, I learned that Puffy was born in July of 2003, no one knew his exact day he was born. Puffy and his siblings were imported from a farm in the country of El Salvador.

Puffy was only a few inches when I met him, he fit in the palm of my hand. We bonded over the first few days together so completely that he knew what I was thinking and seemed to just understand me very well. Puffy knew just what to do and what I expected of him. I call meeting Puffy and bringing him home the best day of my life! Nothing, or nobody, or any other pet I ever had felt as right to me, or displayed the affection, love or understanding that Puffy did, and he was like that from the very start at two months of age.

CHAPTER TWO

Where No Iguana Has Gone Before

Daily life with Puffy was a joy! Iguanas like routine, and he had his breakfast early in the morning around the same time everyday. Puffy ate from his white seashell each morning and throughout the day. His diet as a baby was different than when he was fully grown. Iguanas are herbivores and foliavores. They only eat leaves, stems, certain vegetables and some flowers. Puffy's vegetables and tofu cubes were cut into very small pieces. He had water available to him at all times.

<u>Puffy's Diet as a Baby</u>
- Collard greens
- Turnip greens
- Mustard greens
- Dandelion greens
- Yellow squash
- Bok Choy

- Spring Mix
- Green beans
- Hibiscus flowers
- Rose petals
- Carrots
- Kale
- Apricots (his favorite fruit)
- Apple
- Blueberries
- Pears
- Cantaloupe
- Honeydew
- Tofu Cubes

All Organic Whenever Possible.

Puffy only got a few of these items per day.

As Puffy matured, he ate from a plate on the kitchen floor.

I discovered that Puffy loved organic butternut squash baby food in pouches; I would mix a pouch in with his food daily, he loved it!

Sometimes I would add a little of the organic fruit mixes (for babies) to his meals. One of the following per day:

- Butternut squash/Pear
- Apple/Apricot
- Apple/Blueberry

- Strawberry/Raspberry
- Raspberry/Pear

Puffy was only fed food that was sold bagged. I never fed him loose produce, for sanitary reasons. I would make sure to wash my hands with antibacterial soap and water while preparing his meals and before serving them to him.

Puffy was introduced to traveling at an early age. He indeed went places with me that no iguana has gone before! I took him to department stores, malls, grocery stores, bookstores, the beaches in Florida, bike week in Daytona Beach, Florida, record stores, clothing stores, jewelry shops, furniture stores, hotels, flea market, exotic animal pet stores and reptile expos.

Not once was Puffy a problem in any place I took him. At first, he was on an iguana leash but he held on to me. Later on, he loved being escorted around held, just like you would hold a baby! Some people you see only one time, they give you their "words of wisdom," if you will, and you never see them again. However, they leave their mark, and you remember their words years later. Like the woman who told Puffy "Welcome to the world!" on our first walk together. The man in a flea market in Florida who said "He's going to be great!" This was when Puffy was still only two months of age. Little did that man realize that his saying came true!

Puffy traveled cross-country with my boyfriend, Richard, and I five times. He actually tried to drive the motorhome himself, putting his front paws on the steering wheel! His back paws wouldn't reach the gas or break pedals, but Puffy's paws made the motions! It was incredible! We went from Florida, Texas, Arizona and also California. Puffy was well adjusted to the motorhome, sleeping in the shower or on one of the countertops. Puffy loved looking out at the scenery in every state we passed through or stayed in!

He also made trips in the car or truck, and seemed to enjoy traveling. In hotels, Puffy would sleep behind the pillow, usually behind my head. Several times he enjoyed sleeping on my chest and stomach! Puffy's facial expressions while on these journeys were of happiness and enjoyment! There were always people stopping to take pictures of us wherever we went! Puffy loved posing for the camera; he would really ham it up!

Puffy loved watching movies with Richard and me, he would sit on my head, or on Richard's shoulders. I remember he watched the entire movie "Sunset Boulevard" without even moving! He seemed so fascinated by the acting. Puffy was also attracted to bright colors and good music. He enjoyed watching a good music video every once and awhile. Like us, Puffy liked a good romantic comedy as well: "School of Rock," "Sister Act One," "Sister Act Two," and "Love Actually" were of his list of favorites!

Puffy actually lived in a real haunted house for a short time with me. This was a house in Florida that Richard and I rented without a warning from the rental agent. Puffy was very protective of me, and also quite psychic. I heard the ghosts in this house and Puffy actually saw them! Iguanas can see ultraviolet light, the colors beyond our color spectrum and the spirit world. Puffy was extremely agitated in this house. He would look to the sides and back of me, biting at the air, ready to pounce on the invisible-to-our-eyes residents. He would jump at the air as if the other worldly residents in this house were a threat to us. He would follow their movements with his eyes; Puffy saw the ghosts and was watching them.

Since iguanas have no vocal cords, they can't talk. However, Puffy would somehow force air into his lungs and could make grunting sounds. He was probably trying to tell the ghosts to go away and leave us alone! There were times when Puffy would make grunting sounds of happiness when I held him. If only he was able to talk! I myself had occasions in this house where I heard some of these spirits. One morning at 5am, when I was still in bed, I heard the most beautiful singing close to my left ear. It sounded like the voice of a lady who could really sing! What a lovely voice she had!

At night in every room of this house, I would often hear the voices of many men talking. The words were extremely muffled and sounded like they were coming from somewhere very far away. These happenings didn't particularly bother me, but since Puffy was so upset in this house, we moved out shortly after. I thought I would include these little incidents, since nothing of the sort ever happened again in any other place we lived.

Chapter Three

Nighttime and Bedtime

As previously mentioned, my impression from Puffy at the pet store was "talk to me" and "tuck me in at bedtime!" I did just that throughout his whole life! We had specific bedtime routines together that started on Puffy's first night with me. Puffy would sometimes sleep up high on the kitchen cabinets as he matured. I would climb one of his stepladders to the top, talk to him and pet him. Then, lights out for the night!

When he was still a baby, I would open Puffy's cage up at bedtime, talk to him and pet him goodnight. He often would lick my hand and do his open-and-close eyes routine with me all the while he had a very happy, smiling expression on his face! I would then turn the light and heat lamps off for the night. The rooms Puffy slept in were kept warm at night, via the furnace and space heaters. A nighttime temperature of at least 85°F was preferred by us both!

Iguanas hunker down for the night at sundown everyday. Puffy would choose his sleeping position and get on with it! Here are the exact words I made up that I would talk to Puffy every evening, no matter where we were, at home, or on one of our travels. I made these words up on the spot, spontaneously in Roseland, Florida. Puffy's first home with me was in a mobile home in Roseland, Florida. Here are my words from my heart to Puffy:

My nighttime ritual with Puffy

I wish you the very best of everything, my darling Puffy.
All the best to you and for you, darling Puffy, always.
I love you Puffy. I love you very much.
Hang in there, we'll make it together, we'll get through this together.
Have patience with everything, Puffy. Have patience with
me. Continue on, you're doing excellent.
You're my divine companion, my companion lizard. God brought us together
at just the right time. He'll keep us together in this life and the next.
God Gave me a little bit of himself when he gave you to me.
I tell God you are the most magnificent creature he ever created and you are!
Puffy we'll have a beautiful life together!
You'll have your own sofa (he did) and your own table and chairs (he did).
Whatever I can do to keep you happy, you know I'll do it Puffy.
I'll always take the very best care of you I can (I did).
Every minute with you Puffy, is like being in heaven!
Just being with you Puffy is like being in heaven.
Puffy, we'll enjoy zillions of beautiful sunrises and sunsets together. We'll
enjoy all the beauty the world has to offer, you and I together.

We won't be alone physically in the house tonight, Puffy, but
we will always be alone together, you and I.
I'll be telling you, "That's a good boy Puffy, my precious boy!"
Thank you for a spectacular Saturday (saying whatever day it was) September 27th
(saying the current month and day) in this year of 2003 (saying the current year).
Congratulations, you made it a wonderful day as only you can make it, Puffy.
Pleasant dreams Puffy, dream beautiful dreams for us!
Remember what I told you so many times when we were in Roseland:
No matter where we go,
No matter where we end up,
We'll always be together,
And I'll always love you.

Don't think that Puffy didn't understand this! He showed remarkable responses to the words, facial expressions and body movements that expressed the acceptance of my love for him. It has been quite amazing to me that Puffy chose to sleep in different rooms of the house and in different positions as well! This was mostly in the last house we lived in. Puffy was a full-time "free-roamer "then. I started counting when we first moved in and the total was 927 different ways and places in the house!

9/27 is our anniversary, when we first met at the exotic animal pet store in Florida!

Chapter Four

Daylight and Morning

Our daylight and morning routines together were nothing short of pleasure for us both! Wherever Puffy would have slept, I would go to him at dawn every day, pet him and talk to him. He would spend a long time with his eyes closed, a blissful look on his face, a sure sign of contentment. He was already awake for the day at sunrise. He would lick my hand and wait for me to pick him up. Depending on the time of the year, I would walk around the house with Puffy in the winter for an hour. In summer, I would take him outdoors in the sunshine whenever it was warm and sunny enough.

Puffy had a sun cage built into the kitchen window in Roseland, Florida and in other homes we lived in. He loved going in and out for real sunshine in the morning! A UVB heat lamp was on the kitchen countertop waiting for him when Puffy decided he had enough sunshine for a while. He would bask under the light while I prepared his breakfast. Throughout his life, Puffy loved when I would hand feed him "samples" of his food!

Puffy was introduced to morning showers on his first whole day with me, after our walks, he would enjoy an evening shower as well. This not only provided additional humidity which all tropical lizards love, but also kept him clean. I believe a lot of my success in keeping Puffy alive for 17 years was due to strict sanitary measures: his cage, food and water bowls and all places he walked were kept clean everyday. A piece of paper towel with some liquid anti-bacterial soap was used in the shower for him, I was careful to avoid his head and eyes. Puffy was thoroughly rinsed off with water when done. As a baby, I would hold him while giving him his shower.

Puffy worked out his own routine as an adult. He would stretch out on one of his ladders I placed in the bathtub. In stall showers, Puffy stretched out on the shower floor, placing his head on the shower edge. After his morning shower, Puffy would go back into his own room. When he was a baby, he would go back into his cage. I would talk to Puffy about all kinds of things, from my life before he was in it, to my hopes and dreams for us.

Since UVB light is so important for an iguana's health and well-being, Puffy would spend his daylight hours in the sun, under his UVB bulb, or on a bird tree placed by a sunny window. The window was left open and a screen was placed in it. He even had UVB light and fixture set up for him in the motor home. Various UVB bulbs were used over the years, I found the "PowerSun" by Zoomed Labs to be the best bulb for Puffy. It has UVB and UVA light plus heat, all in one bulb.

I would place the 100-watt bulb 18"-24" inches above his basking spot. The 160-watt bulb would be 24"-36" away from his basking spot whenever a stronger light and heat was needed. On our outdoor excursions, Puffy liked to be carried around on my chest and shoulders like a baby. It was a sight to see! Here are my exact words that I spoke to Puffy every morning, once again, I made these words up spontaneously, on the spot, in Roseland, Florida. They are completely from my heart to Puffy.

My daylight and morning ritual with Puffy

Good morning, my darling Puffy.
Happy Saturday (saying whatever day it was) September 27th,
2003 (saying the correct month, day and year).
I hope you had a wonderful night's sleep!
I hope you dreamed beautiful dreams for us!
You're my darling little Puffy, my darling little Po! (One of the nicknames I gave Puffy)
You're simply the best, Puffy, in any world or universe, past, present or future!
You're very special, Puffy!
You're awesome, incredible, remarkable, outstanding, you're exceptional, Puffy!
You'll always be my little sweetheart!
This is my guy!
This is my boy!
I'm so happy to be with you, Puffy!
It's so good to be with you, it's wonderful to be with you Puffy!
Let's make this a great day together!
I'll be chilling out with you today, Puffy!
(If I was going out that day without Puffy, I would say to him…)
I'm always with you spiritually, Puffy If I'm not with your physically.

There were lots of places I took Puffy, especially when he was a baby. Even as an adult I would take him along on errands, but most grocery stores forbid him to enter in. Little did they know just how clean and well behaved Puffy was, better than most of the customers, or in some cases all the customers!

CHAPTER FIVE

No Passing Fancy

Puffy was so physically appealing, I would like to talk to you about some of what made him so handsome! First, Puffy's coloration was splendid. A bright green as a baby, Puffy's coloring changed over the years to even more spectacular hues! He was made up of a light green, grey, black, brown, bright orange, turquoise and spots of blue. His jowls (male as adults have large jowls) were a beautiful mother-of-pearl color, like that of a seashell.

In breeding season, two more colors appeared, rust and peach. His orange coloration became more pronounced, like the bright orange of a pumpkin. I would call Puffy "The Great Pumpkin" and "Pumpkin Face" when he displayed the brilliant orange during these times (usually October-March every year). Puffy's behavior during breeding season was truly remarkable. He never became aggressive towards me; he remained the sweet, gentle guy he always was.

Puffy would bite his hard plastic food plate, an acceptable form of aggression for me, leaving dents in the plate! Iguanas have sharp teeth! During breeding season, Puffy would enjoy sleeping at the side of my bed, or above my head and pillow. He loved a lot of affection and attention from me during breeding season. Puffy abandoned sleeping in his cage or in his room whenever I was ill, and after I had an operation on my legs. He would spend all of his time with me, and what a comfort he was!

Puffy had a long, slender, graceful body; he was filled out just right. No wonder he loved posing for pictures! Puffy had a very beautiful, sweet looking face. At times he reminded me of a mythical god, especially when he had his eyes closed. In a way, I suppose, he was more in touch with the divine then we would like to think. Puffy's "windows of the soul," his eyes, were exceptionally gorgeous, and very expressive. His eyes had a dreamy quality to them. Puffy with the dreamy, faraway eyes, yet they're so close. Puffy knew he could always be himself with me, and I knew that I could always be myself with him.

Chapter Six

Music, Maestro

Puffy enjoyed music a lot, and he had his favorite songs! He grew up listening to easy listening, smooth jazz, Bob Marley, and rock and roll. Puffy's favorite song was "The Closer I get to You" sung by Roberta Flack and Donny Hathaway. Every Saturday morning, I would sing "Come Saturday Morning" to him, a lovely song sung by the Sandpipers. He loved this tune and really got into it whenever he would hear it on the radio! I would join him; this happens to be one of my favorite songs as well. Puffy showed interesting responses to music, and I believe he actually understood the words.

Two beautiful new age instrumentals really moved Puffy and I a lot. "New Beginnings" and "Calming Skies" by Steve Wingfield are awesome songs that can put you into another state of consciousness. Both songs are on the CD "Time for Wellness" by Steve Wingfield. Puffy enjoyed songs from all decades, as Frank Sinatra singing "Moonlight in Vermont," "Christmas Is" by the Percy Faith Orchestra, and "Our Winter Love" by Bill Purcell. He would boogie on down to all the songs by Bob Marley, the Beatles and AC/DC! He had good music taste!

Puffy would often rest his face on my cheek when we listened to the tear-jerker songs. He was able to tune into the emotions and feelings I felt. The song "I Can't Tell You Why" by the Eagles often brought a tear to my eyes, and Puffy understood completely. Puffy's reactions were more like those of a mammal. For a reptile, he was very advanced!

CHAPTER SEVEN

I Say a Little Prayer for You

I am not a particularly "religious" individual in that sense of the word, but after being with Puffy, one can't help but believe in God. Here is a prayer I made up to Jesus, by whom all things were created. I looked at Puffy as one of God's creations, to me, the very best he ever did, and ever will.

"To Jesus, Concerning Puffy"

Thank you Jesus, for Puffy.
To me, he is a blessing and a miracle. He is the most magnificent
creature you ever created, in my opinion.
Please bless Puffy every day of his wonderful, long-lived life.
Let Puffy know how much I love him, and let him return the love to me.
Let Puffy and I continue to grow in our special love and relationship with each other.
Let Puffy continue to grow to be the most handsome, the most gorgeous, the most
beautiful, the best looking, the sweetest, the most calm, the most relaxed, the
gentlest, the most mellow, the most pain-free at all times, the most non-aggressive,
even in the breeding season, the most long-lived, the happiest, the healthiest, the
best all-around iguana he can be. That's how much I love Puffy, Jesus.
It is my fondest prayer to you, Jesus, that Puffy and I be together
forever, not just in this world, but with you in the next.
I pray in your name, Jesus.
Thank you.

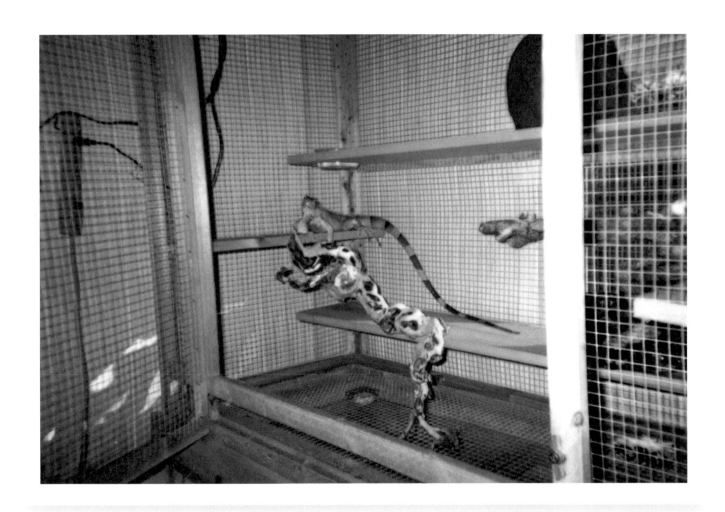

Chapter Eight

The Beginning of the End

It is very important that green iguanas have a yearly exam by a qualified exotic animal vet, Puffy received the best medical care over the years, from a check up, to regular nail trims and even a few surgeries. Puffy was treated by several different exotic animal vets depending on where we lived at the time he needed to see a vet.

Puffy survived a motor home fire in December of 2012. He managed to get out through a broken window. Puffy was found near the burned down motor home. He didn't try to run away. Whoever found him called animal control, and he was taken there. I picked him up from there the following morning. Puffy was very fortunate to still be alive. He had some injuries and had several inches removed from his tail. He was treated for smoke inhalation as well by an exotic vet. Ketamine was given to Puffy so he could be asleep during the procedure.

Various vets cured Puffy of flagellate infections; flagellates are a type of internal parasite. Flagyl was given orally and I would mix it into his food. Flagyl is also used for certain infections in humans as well. A wonderful exotic vet in Florida cured Puffy of a nasty case of mouth rot. The problem started from a bite of a female iguana, the bite never healed up and became worse. Puffy was asleep under the anesthetic ketamine for the entire surgery. Our favorite vet bears mention here. Puffy liked her a lot, and vice-versa. Dr. Alyssa Scagnelli is an excellent exotic animal vet working from a clinic in Gilbert, Arizona. She has treated Puffy from 2018, when we moved to Arizona, up until February 14, 2020, Puffy's last visit to the vet. Dr. Scagnelli has 9 lizards of her own, two of them being green iguanas, she has a great "bedside manner" with Puffy.

On February 14, 2020, Puffy was diagnosed with a spider bite, weakness and weight loss. A variety of tests were done on Puffy. He had an exam, x-rays and blood work. Nothing showed up to account for his symptoms. His blood work was normal, the x-rays showed a broken rib that healed by itself and Puffy's exam showed nothing abnormal. I had no idea that Puffy was on his way out, neither did Dr. Scagnelli. Over several months, I was in touch with Dr. Scagnelli over the phone. The weakness in Puffy was getting worse. He was like a ragdoll when I held him or took him for a walk. Puffy spent a lot of time with his eyes closed and he didn't look happy. Puffy still had a great appetite and he never turned down his meals. Most iguanas refuse to eat when ill.

I did mention to Dr. Scagnelli that Puffy went into an abnormally brief breeding season, starting on Thursday, January 16th, 2020, and lasting only a month. She advised me not to be worried about it. Puffy started having trouble walking and moving his head properly. At that point, I should have realized that something was very wrong. Indeed, something was very wrong. Puffy's body was shutting down, little by little. Throughout all this, Puffy remained the sweet, gentle, loving guy he was. He still loved going out for his early morning walks in the sunshine. He loved being held a lot, petted, spoken to and hand fed.

Green iguanas are experts at concealing their pain. This is a survival technique. In the rainforests where they come from, predators are everywhere, hunting them down for lunch.

Puffy did an excellent job at hiding just how serious his health problem was. He stayed mostly in his room under his UVB light, sleeping at night in his closet. He would choose different positions and places in his room to hang out in. May 25th, 2020, was the very last time that Puffy walked into my room to spend the night with me. For the next several months, he would only sleep in his room.

CHAPTER NINE

The Last Year of Puffy's Life

This chapter will go over the events of Puffy's life for the year 2020. I will touch briefly on the day he passed on. Tuesday, December 31st, 2019, New Years Eve, Puffy spent the night with me in my room. He slept at the side of my bed, like he used to do when I was ill. We rang in 2020 together.

On Friday, January 3rd, 2020, Puffy performed a talented dance in the stall shower! The water was not on and he was not trying to climb. Puffy put his front paws on the shower wall, standing up on his back legs. He then actually did some dancing, moving his back legs in a rhythm even Fred Astaire would have envied! I was trying to teach Puffy how to dance throughout his entire life. Looks like I didn't need to teach him anything! Puffy demonstrated a marvelous sense of rhythm! We danced together for short times over the years, now Puffy was doing a solo! How I wish I had a camera on hand to capture this, it was truly amazing!

Thursday, January 16th, 2020 was the start of Puffy's last breeding season. It only lasted into February. Through Friday, January 31st, 2020 through Tuesday, February 4th, 2020, Puffy stayed in my room by the side of my bed. He only came out for meals in the kitchen, his showers, and walks with me outside. May 25th, 2020 was the very last time Puffy ever slept in my room. Our morning walks for 2020 started on Saturday, May 2nd, the temperature in the deep freeze here was finally warm enough to walk Puffy outside. There was plenty of early morning sunshine for Puffy to enjoy.

On Thursday, February 13th, 2020, Puffy enjoyed going to the mall in Mesa where we lived before moving to a colder area of Arizona. He had fun going to the stores and slept behind my pillow in the hotel room. On Friday, February 14th, 2020, Valentine's Day, Puffy had his last visit with Dr. Scagnelli. We then proceeded to another mall in Mesa. Puffy had a wonderful time, and I was so happy to be with my Valentine!

No one had any idea that this was Puffy's last trip to the malls and stores. The next several months, Puffy and I followed the same routine. We did our daylight and nighttime rituals, Puffy had his showers and I would fix him the best breakfasts I could. Puffy looked forward to his walks each morning. I would carry him like a baby, go up the hills outside the house, down the back round road, until we reached a private drive. We walked the drive two or three times, then went back onto the back round road again. Puffy and I left the house early enough each morning to avoid any major traffic. People in cars or on bicycles would stop me to ask questions about Puffy and to take pictures of Puffy on their cellphones!

It must have been a sight to see from the highway! It was not very common to see a lady holding an iguana almost as big as she is like he was a baby and walking with him! I would sing to Puffy and talk with him a lot. He seemed to enjoy the singing and I know that he understood all that I spoke to him about. In this area, there are a variety of weeds that produce beautiful colorful flowers from May through the end of September. I would point out these lovely weed flowers to Puffy, he enjoyed looking at them! Some of these flowers almost didn't look real. One light bluish green weed was pretty enough without the flowers. When in bloom, it had large white flowers that looked like paper. The back roads had lavender weed flowers with yellow centers, along with rows of dazzling yellow sunflowers.

A series of pink, blue and orange weed flowers looked a lot like morning glories. Our morning walks were almost like being in a botanical garden. One back road led back to the main road. Puffy and I would cross over to the right side, the side called "The Sunny Side for the Sunshine boy!" I would sing to Puffy " On The Bright Side Of The Road," a song by Van Morrison. Further up the hill were some spectacular bright red weed flowers with bright yellow centers. They looked like bugles, and I would say to Puffy "lets see the bugles today," he understood exactly what I was talking about! With Puffy's attraction to bright colors, he really enjoyed seeing these lovely weed flowers each morning!

We would walk for an hour and a half, and head on back to the house. Once inside the house, Puffy would have a morning shower and eat his breakfast in the kitchen. This is Puffy's diet when he was an adult. I still continued to cut his vegetables up very fine for him. Puffy no longer ate tofu cubes, fruit or organic baby food. The only organic baby food he would eat was the butternut squash. I would mix a pouch into his food each day; he wouldn't eat anything without it! Puffy was fed only organic vegetables sold in bags his entire life. Bottled drinking water was sprinkled over his food. A pinch of "Herptivite" multivitamin powder for reptiles was mixed into his meals.

As an adult, Puffy lost his taste for carrots, kale, dandelion greens, tofu cubes and fruit. The only fruit he would occasionally gobble down was apricots. One time I hand fed Puffy 6 apricots cut up for him. He stood up on his back legs and took the apricots from my fingers, much like a dog would do!

Puffy's Diet as an Adult
One pouch of organic butternut squash baby food per day mixed into his food.

A Few of These Per Day
Collard Greens
Turnip Greens
Mustard Greens
Green Beans
Sugar Snap Peas
Snow Peas
Hibiscus Flowers
Rose Petals
Yellow Squash
Spring Mix
Bok Choy
Apricots

Bottled Drinking water

A small pinch of "Herptivite" (multivitamin powder for reptiles mixed into his food)

Puffy enjoyed another lukewarm shower after breakfast. He would go back into his room and bask under his UVB bulb all day. I would have wonderful conversations with Puffy and played him music all day from the radio or CDs. I did whatever I could to make Puffy as comfortable and as happy as possible. Puffy no longer went out for rides in the car or truck. This was due mostly to living in a cold area in Arizona. The temperature was kept at least 85 degrees in the house. A space heater was on in Puffy's room whenever extra heat was needed.

Saturday, May 2nd, 2020 was the start of our morning walks for the year. Saturday, October 24th, 2020, was Puffy's last walk outside with me. It was too cold to take him outside anymore. I would still walk Puffy around the house inside for about an hour. I continued talking to him and holding him the way he liked, head on my shoulder, body on my chest! After all, Puffy was way too big to sit on top of my head anymore! He tried it a few times and managed to stay on top of my head while I walked him around the rooms of the house!

Every July, Puffy received a Happy Birthday greeting each day of the month. The exact day in July he was born was not known. I had no clue that July of 2020 was the last time I would ever wish Puffy a Happy Birthday. All of those lovely weed flowers were gone by the time Puffy and I enjoyed our last walk outside together. Not long after, Puffy would be gone as well. On Monday morning of November 9th, 2020, everything started out as usual, and ended with Puffy checking out of this world.

CHAPTER Ten

The Worst Day of My Life

I would like to start this chapter by letting you know about two "premonition" dreams I experienced. Both dreams occurred in October of 2020, one month before my world fell apart. The first dream found me in an outdoor setting, at night. I was in a place I have never seen before. The streets had a carnival type of atmosphere. I was with people I have never seen before when awake. All of a sudden, I realized Puffy was not there! I panicked severely yelling out, "Where's Puffy? I need to go find him!" I started running away from the dream people, down weird, twisting, turning streets that really looked like an amusement park now. I was crying and was terrified because I couldn't find Puffy anywhere, Of course, I woke up at this point, sweating, my heart racing, and still feeling panic. I ran into Puffy's room to make sure he was there. He was still fast asleep.

The second dream was much more direct. This one was about a week apart from the first one. I was back in that horrible carnival place from the first dream. It was a nightmare. The same people were there again. I have no idea who they are. These people are complete strangers to me, both in the dream and in waking life. I asked the people "Where's Puffy?

What am I doing here without Puffy?" One person said to me, "He's with your sister." I yelled out, "I have to catch a plane to New York immediately! She doesn't know how to take care of him!" I experienced the most horrible severe panic anyone can experience.

I woke up in a waking state of severe panic, sweating, my heart racing like when I woke up from the first dream. This time, I had a terrible sense of dread and doom. I ran again into Puffy's room, once again, Puffy was still fast asleep, was I glad to see him! Let me inform you all that my sister passed away 10 years earlier. She had a heart attack and was found dead on the floor of her apartment in New York.

Even with these two dreams as a warning, what I could I, or anyone else have done to extend Puffy's life? The real nightmare had started; it was a day just like any other. The dawn of Monday, November 9th, 2020 found me in Puffy's room. We were doing our usual daylight routines. Puffy had his morning shower. This day, he spent a lot of time in my room while I prepared his breakfast. He walked out of his room, leaving his UVB light that he would bask under, and marched right into my room. He came out on his own, walking down the hallway into the kitchen. Puffy jumped into the air as if to climb onto me in the hallway. He has a big grin all over his face! He didn't look ill at all. Puffy climbed halfway up his white metal ladder in the dining area very well. He started losing control of his muscles and fell off the ladder. I picked him up and placed him in front of his breakfast.

Puffy enjoyed his last meal this morning, as he always did. I kissed him and petted him when he was done eating. I held him and spoke to him for a while. We proceeded to the shower, Puffy stretched himself out, head resting on the edge, like always. Puffy looked up at me with pure love all over his face. Not that he had never looked at me with love before; this was something different entirely. I'll never forget it. This was a look that even the finest love movie couldn't match. Once again, I wish I had a camera handy to film it.

After Puffy had his lukewarm shower, I kissed him and carried him back to his room. Just like any other morning, I placed Puffy under his UVB bulb for his basking time. Around 10:00 am, I started to notice a foul odor. It was coming from Puffy's room. I went into his room and found Puffy in his closet, lying in a pile of horrible smelling poop. Puffy was in a state of shock. His eyes were wide open in fear. He wasn't moving. I placed him in the shower again and cleaned him up. I quickly cleaned and disinfected his closet. Dr. Scagnelli is several hours away from where we live, too far away to rush Puffy there. I was given a referral to a vet about an hour away.

Richard and I rushed Puffy to this vet that was closer. By this time, Puffy was drifting in and out of consciousness. Richard asked Puffy to "hang in there." Puffy opened his eyes at the sound of his name, and then collapsed. I held Puffy on my lap, trying my best to stay as calm as I could. Puffy was already unconscious when we entered the vet's office. Puffy was placed on a heart monitor and a breathing machine. He lasted for 7 minutes, then the lines on the machine went flat. Puffy had no heartbeat at all. He wasn't breathing at all, either. My whole world came to an abrupt halt. Puffy was pronounced deceased at 2:37pm, 7 minutes after he entered the vet's office.

We brought Puffy home. I gave him a shower and held him and loved him for a long time. I don't want to talk too much about my crying. I placed Puffy's body back in his room under his UVB bulb. I turned the light off at sundown, just like I always did. Puffy's eyes were partially open. I had a feeling that he might still be alive. For the next three days, I went about business as if Puffy were still living. When I held him, he has no muscle tone in his head or neck. The muscles were totally wasted away. His head would droop and move around as if it were going to fall off. His facial expression was one of horrible sadness.

On Thursday, November 12th, 2020, Richard and I took Puffy to Dr. Scagnelli. At my request, Dr. Scagnelli said that she would try and revive Puffy, if it were possible. Puffy was pronounced deceased, but it was worth trying. Puffy was placed on a heart and breathing machine. He was given injections to start his heart again. Nothing brought Puffy back to life, not even my love for him. I was totally heart broken and cried in Dr. Scagnelli's arms. At my request, Dr. Scagnelli agreed to do an autopsy to find the cause of Puffy's passing on. I left Puffy in the clinic's freezer.

For the first time in 17 years, I went home without Puffy. The autopsy results were revealed to me over the phone a few weeks later. Puffy had an enlarged heart with scar tissue. He died from a stroke. At the present time, there are no tests to check for heart disease in reptiles. Puffy's problem was most likely genetic, as it is in humans. Living in a cold climate after being raised in a warm, sunny, humid environment might have made the situation worse. The spider bite Puffy had was completely healed up, and was not a cause for his death.

Just as in humans, having a heart condition wasted Puffy's muscles away and caused significant weight loss and weakness, despite Puffy's good appetite. A warm, sunny, humid environment might have extended Puffy's life a year at the most. With a heart problem, and the fact that he was 17 years of age he wouldn't have lasted more than another year, at the most. I lost the only one for me to death; I still can't believe that this happened. Why? Why Puffy? I would do anything to have him back alive and healthy again. What to do with Puffy's body? There is no method yet of preserving it.

A small fortune would enable me to purchase a private plot and give Puffy an elaborate burial, casket and all. All of Puffy's organs were found to be normal at the time of his passing. There were no health problems found, other then the heart condition. I feel that Puffy could have lived longer. I love him, I always will, and he is missed and thought about constantly. Once in a lifetime, there is someone who comes into your life and gives it meaning and happiness. This was what Puffy did for me. I am grateful for the 17 wonderful years with him. Puffy gave me a reason for living and made my life worth living in a way that no one or nothing else could.

CHAPTER ELEVEN

Love Eternal

So where is Puffy now? Each religion would give you a different opinion. The essence that is Puffy, his soul, will forever be with me and live on. This is what I believe, and Puffy and I were, and still are, bonded together on the soul level, and it's forever. I still do our morning and evening talks together, just as if Puffy is still here with me. From wherever Puffy is now, I like to think that he can hear me somehow, and remember our love!

I know that where Puffy is, he no longer has pain of any kind, and has no needs or wants like hunger, thirst, being too hot or too cold. That's better then what most of us face daily, being alive. The only catch is that Puffy is not conscious or living, at least not the way we know it.

"To you, my darling Puffy"

Puffy, wherever you are now, I hope you are always happy.

Please don't forget me, my beloved Puffy.

Let's recognize each other again, and find each other again, no matter what form we will be in.

All my love always, darling Puffy.

Thank you for being with me 17 years. I wish it could have been many more years.

I'll see you and be with you again 'Po, next time it will be forever, with no separations.

I found what I was looking for in life, in you, Puffy.

Puffy
July, 2003 – November 9th, 2020

Chapter Twelve

Epilogue

It is my hope that what is written in this book will inspire and help you see your own pet in a different light. Particularly if your pet happens to be an iguana! Give your iguana a chance to show you life in a fuller way. Take the time to get to know your iguana's own special personality. Show him how much you love and appreciate him.

Every iguana has his or her own unique personality; just as us humans have our own unique, individual make up. It is my hope for you, also, that if you are thinking of getting an iguana that you find one as special to you as Puffy is to me. There are many fine books on iguana care, but it is up to you to provide the love and devotion to your iguana, as I did with Puffy.

Then, watch what happens to your life.

Best wishes,
Laura

CHAPTER THIRTEEN

An Update

You could call this wishful fulfillment if you like, but I prefer to think it was really him!

Yes, Puffy was here on the morning of Monday, January 25th, 2021, in a "dream." I use the word "dream" lightly, as I was fully conscious when this miracle occurred. From the ceiling in Puffy's room appeared a series of gorgeous specks of very bright multi-colored lights. They just materialized out of the air. The lights formed themselves into… Puffy! Puffy appeared under the spot where he basked under his UVB bulb. He was stretched out facing the window. Puffy turned his head and smiled at me with the most loving expression on his face! He looked fully alive and healthy. How gorgeous he looked and how happy I was to see him again!

In this so-called "dream," I was standing in the doorway of Puffy's room. I was observing this miracle without entering his room. I did not run in to touch him. For those of us who believe it's possible, Puffy might actually have been back in his room for a few minutes! Who is really to say? I spoke to Puffy in soft, gentle tones without going into his room to pet him. He looked happy to see me! The atmosphere changed and I "woke up" after this, and of course at that point, Puffy's room was empty once again.

Chapter Fourteen

Burned and Urned

I made the decision to have Puffy's body cremated after giving the situation much thought. Puffy is no longer in his body, or in this world. He wouldn't feel anything or even realize what happened. Cremation is an opportunity to have the physical part of Puffy with me for the rest of my life. On Friday, March 12th, 2021, Puffy was privately picked up from Dr. Scagnelli's clinic. I had arranged for a private ceremony where Puffy would be the only one undergoing cremation at the time.

On Saturday, March 13th, 2021 at 7:53am, Puffy's body was reduced to ashes; his bones were ground down to powder by a separate procedure. Puffy was given a beautiful, hand carved rosewood urn to rest in. On Tuesday, March 16th, 2021, Puffy was driven back to Dr. Scagnelli's clinic; he arrived at 10:04am. Friday, April 30th, 2021, Richard and I picked up Puffy's remains in the urn. At 12:30pm, I held what was left of Puffy's body and we took him home.

When Puffy was living, my hand would tingle when I pet him! It was a lovely, warm feeling, like when the sunshine warms your hand. It was as if Puffy's energy and essence were being transferred to me. This same sensation occurred when I held the urn with Puffy's ashes and bones in it! I could sense the essence of what Puffy was! It was sending warm, wonderful tingling sensations in my hand! Puffy's ashes and bones are in a little bag of plastic inside of the urn. The urn is a beautiful rosewood square box around 7"x4" with lovely hand carved flowers on top of the urn. I could still sense Puffy, even if his body is gone. The love we had together remains alive always. I have the urn right by my bedside. The soul and spirit of Puffy will always be with me, and my soul and spirit will always be with him.

What you have just read in these pages is a work of non-fiction.
Everything written in this book really happened.

ABOUT THE AUTHOR

Laura Miller, born and raised in New York City. She graduated high
school in a specialized art school and went on to take 2 and a half
years at a junior college studying fashion. Worked as a commercial
artist for many years. She writes her own music, has her own CD
but hasn't published anything yet. She believes that when the body
goes, the essence of what God made us, our soul, every living thing
continues to live on.

Printed in the United States
by Baker & Taylor Publisher Services